The 7 Laws of Network Marketing

By Chris Widener
and Anthony Powell

Made for Success
PUBLISHING

Made for Success Publishing
P.O. Box 1775
Issaquah, WA 98027

The 7 Laws of Network Marketing

Designed by DeeDee Heathman

Library of Congress Cataloging-in-Publication data

Widener, Chris and Powell, Anthony
The 7 Laws of Network Marketing / Chris
Widener and Anthony Powell.
p. cm.
ISBN-13: 978-1-61339-904-0 (pbk.)
LCCN: 206921238

To contact the author or publisher please email
service@MadeforSuccess.net or call +1 425 657 0300.

Made for Success Publishing is an
imprint of Made for Success, inc.

Printed in the United States of America

WHAT PEOPLE ARE SAYING ABOUT "THE SEVEN LAWS OF NETWORK MARKETING"

"Chris has written a book that will accelerate your business dramatically as it truly gets to the HEART of what this business is all about with this amazing story. It brilliantly walks you through, step by step in the story, on what WORKS and what the TRUTH is about Success in network marketing. Often we get distracted to what REALLY matters for success in our profession and he has NAILED it unlike any other book of it's kind out there. Epic. Brilliant. It MUST be part of your library!"

~Dr. Doug Firebaugh, CEO, DFTI

"The 7 Laws of Network Marketing is an extraordinary little book, written in a parable form that makes learning these foundational lessons fun and easy. This book will teach you the core principles of a successful network marketing business. Get it. Read it. Apply it!"

~Eric Worre, Founder, Network Marketing Pro

"Chris Widener and Anthony Powell do a brilliant job of teaching the 7 Laws of Network Marketing in this new book! I was engaged from the first few words and devoured it in one sitting.

What a great read for someone wanting to learn… and do so in the most fun way possible!

The story told in this book will have you understanding how to apply these 7 Laws in no time!"

~Todd Falcone, Author, Speaker and Network Marketing Trainer

"I found myself nodding in agreement and loving the wisdom on every page of this book. The laws are so powerful and undeniable; there is no doubt in my mind this book will be on the shelf of every network marketing professional."

~Andrea Waltz, Co-Author, *Go for No!*

"The Seven Laws of Network Marketing is real life. The story that Chris and Anthony tell is a story that plays out weekly in the lives of those that have built large network marketing organizations. A chance meeting leads to many coaching and mentoring conversations over a period of time. Lessons are learned and applied. Most top networkers will see a reflection of themselves

in Keller's story as he gets mentored by Tony in this book. It belongs in the library of anyone that is serious about building a great organization."

~Jordan Adler, Network Marketing Millionaire, Author of the Amazon Best Seller, *Beach Money*

"*I love the way Chris and Anthony make the points with a story. These are the exact same principles we have tried to duplicate into our Network Marketing business! These laws have not only helped us become eight-figure earners, but has also helped thousands on our team see massive success as well.*"

~Robert and Donna Fason, Top Income Earners, Team National

"*Chris Widener and Anthony Powell have captured the essence in 'The 7 Laws of Network Marketing' of what it takes to build a viable, enduring network marketing organization. Their storytelling writing style is remarkably captivating and intriguing, keeping the reader in rapt attention. Bravo!*"

~David Humpreys, Founder, Prescription for Freedom

Contents

THE SEVEN LAWS:

It was a beautiful March day in Scottsdale, Arizona, the city Tony Maxwell had moved to a few years ago. It was sunny, not a cloud in the sky and 72 degrees. Tony got out of his 2015 convertible Ferrari Italia 458 and walked into Starbucks. The Starbucks was really busy; it was so busy in fact, that it was about a ten-minute wait for coffee. No problem for Tony, however. He had all the time in the world. Life was good, and he was enjoying every minute of it, even a wait in line for coffee. He was the ultimate optimist, and it had served him well in life.

Inch by inch he made his way to the front of the line. At the counter, he decided to splurge from his regular dark roast drip coffee. *"I'll take a grande, extra hot, extra shot, caramel macchiato, please."*

The young woman at the counter took his payment and apologized in advance, saying, *"I'm sorry, but one of our baristas called in sick so, it will be a few extra minutes."*

"No problem at all," Tony said. He turned away and moved to the side of the counter to wait. He was flipping through his phone, answering the many texts he wakes up to from his many business partners around the world.

He glanced over to his right and saw a young man, maybe 27 years old, looking intensely at his computer. Tony is always looking for new business partners and this guy looked like he was serious about something, so he decided to strike up a conversation.

"Excuse me," Tony said. *"Do you mind if I ask what you are working on? You seem so engaged."*

The young man looked up to see Tony standing over him. He figured Tony was about 45 years old, and he figured exactly right. He seemed nice enough, so he responded. *"Uh, sure. Yeah, so I'm watching training videos on the back end of our website. Trying to learn the new business I just got into."*

"Oh yeah, a new business? What kind of business are you in?"

The young man felt that reluctant fear he gets when people ask him the question. He just never knew how they were going to respond. He knew that it could go either way, but he spits it out anyway. "*I am in a network marketing company.*"

"*You are? How is it going?*" Tony asked.

"*I just started about three months ago, and I'm trying to learn how to do it right. So I guess it isn't going that well yet. I know I just need to learn the secret. Get the key to unlocking success.*"

Tony remembered one of his favorite quotes. "*When the student is ready, the teacher appears.*"

"*That's interesting that you are in network marketing. I am too,*" Tony offered.

"*You are?*" the younger man asked.

"*I am. It's great. I've been in it a while, though.*"

"*What company are you in?*" the young man asked. Tony told him and then asked the same question of him. Tony was familiar with the company.

"*I'm Tony, by the way. What is your name?*" Tony extended his hand. The young man stood up and shook Tony's hand. I'm Keller."

"*Cool name.*"

"*Yeah, my mom named me after my grandfather. It's unique.*" He sat back down. Looking up, he asked, "*So do you do network marketing full time?*"

"*I have a grande, extra hot, extra shot, caramel macchiato, for Tony,*" the barista shouted. Tony turned and grabbed the cup and then brought his attention back to Keller.

"*Yes, I've been full time since about six months after I started. So almost 27 years.*"

"*Wow,*" Keller said admiringly. "*I would love to be able to do that.*"

"*You can. You absolutely can.*" A thought flashed through Tony's mind. And I can teach you. He knew that Keller was in another company and he had no intentions of trying to get him to move over. He was just feeling... generous. The kid just seemed cool to him and sounded like he wants to succeed. "*I'll tell you what... do you live around here?*"

"*Yeah, just a couple miles away. Why?*"

"*I can really help you if you want some help. I've been very successful in this business. How about we swap cell numbers and we can come back here for some coffee and I'll teach you a thing or two. I'll give you some tips that could cut your learning curve way down and*" *get you on the way to not only being full time but killing it in network marketing.*"

"*I would love that,*" Keller said. It's a deal!

"*Just one thing. Before we meet, look me up on the internet. It will tell you more about me. My name is Tony Maxwell. You'll find it interesting.*"

"*For sure. I'll do it,*" Keller promised.

So the two exchanged numbers, Keller went back to work, and Tony re-entered the sun, climbed into his Ferrari, and hit the road. *I hope he calls. That will show if he's serious.*

Keller was sitting at his desk that evening when he remembered the conversation he had with Tony that morning. *Hmmm... I should look him up.*

He did a quick internet search and was surprised at how many results he found. Tens of thousands of search results. Tony even had a Wikipedia page. He clicked it to read more about this seemingly random stranger who had popped into his life. He scanned it briefly.

One of the top income earners of all time in network marketing - top income earner in his company - one of the biggest in the industry - lifetime group volume of product sold nearly

$100 Billion.

Wow. I better get with this guy if he is willing to help me. Keller immediately sent Tony a text to the number he got, and they set up a time to meet at Starbucks the next day.

THE LAW OF SOWING AND REAPING

K eller got to Starbucks early to scope out a good place to sit where he and Tony could have some privacy. Tony arrived right on time and, after getting some coffee, joined Keller in some comfortable stuffed chairs.

"*How's it going, buddy,*" Tony asked.

"*Great! Thanks so much for meeting me. I checked you out online. You have a fantastic business. Who would have thought I would bump into you at my local Starbucks?*"

"*Yes, I've had a good run, that's for sure. And I'm happy to meet with you. You seem like a good guy, and I can give you some good advice. And I want you to know that I am not going to try and recruit you to work with me. That's unethical. I'll help you become successful in your own business. When you are successful, you can pass it on.*"

"*That's awesome! So where do we start,*" Keller asked eagerly.

Tony chuckled. *He wants to get right down to business.*

"*Well, I'm going to teach you the seven laws of network marketing success. That's what I call them. I learned some from mentors and some out of trial and error. It took me years, but these are the laws that work. Apply them, and they'll work for you too.*"

"*Great, what's the first law?*"

"*The first law...*" Tony tilted his head up as though he remembered it fondly. "*The first law is a universal law. It is the law of the ancients. It is a universal law. It is a law that works in almost any situation, any realm, any culture, anywhere really. It comes from the earth. It's as old as the world itself. The very first humans experienced this law.*"

Keller was so intrigued he leaned forward in his chair.

"*It is the law of sowing and reaping. You know the saying, 'you reap what you sow'?*"

"*Sure, of course,*" Keller said.

"*Do you know where that saying comes from?*" Tony asked.

Keller thought. "*No, I guess I don't. But I've heard it forever.*"

"*It actually comes from the Bible. My mentor - we all need mentors, people who teach us - used to tell the story. I keep it on a card in my wallet.*" Tony pulled the paper from his wallet and read it to Keller.

"*A farmer went out to sow his seed. As he was scattering the seed, some fell along the path, and the birds came and ate it up. Some fell on rocky places, where it did not have much soil. It sprang up quickly because the soil was shallow. But when the sun came up, the plants were scorched, and they withered because they had no root. Other seed fell among thorns, which grew up and choked the plants. Still other seed fell on good soil, where it produced a crop - a hundred, sixty or thirty times what was sown. He who has ears, let him hear.*" Matthew 13:3-8 (NIV)

Tony continued. "*This is the first lesson the original humans learned. You put a seed into the ground; you get something back out. It works in all areas of life. You invest money; you get a return. You give love to your spouse; you get love in return. You reap what you sow.*"

"So how does this apply to network marketing? I mean, I think I get it, but tell me more. Help me understand."

"Well, there is the basic message, and there are a few sub-messages, all of which are important. The first is that you reap what you sow. Sowing is talking to people, making presentations, talking to people about your product or services, sharing the business opportunity. Let me ask you, how many people a day are you sharing with? How many people are you sowing into, planting the seed?"

"Every day? Maybe every week. I don't talk to people every day about my business."

"How many people did you talk to yesterday?"

"Yesterday? None. I was watching videos in the back office."

"And how much money did that make you?" Tony had a grin on his face.

Keller got the point and smiled himself with the realization. *"Nothing."*

Tony clapped his hands with one big, loud clap. *"EXACTLY! Nothing. You didn't plant the seed, and therefore you will reap no fruit. You see, some people talk to one person a day. That's good I guess. That's 365 people a year. Let's say that five percent sign up in your* business. That's about 18 people. That's fine. But what if you talked to three people a day? That's over 1000 people a year. Now that five percent is over 50 people in your business. And if you raise that closing rate to eight percent, you're talking 80 people. You have to plant the seed, and you plant the seed by talking to people!"

"That makes total sense. I guess I just get sidetracked sometimes, and sometimes I'm afraid..." His voice trailed off.

"Well, do you have an apple tree in your backyard?"

Keller thought that was a strange question. "No, I don't."

"That means no one ever planted an apple seed there! You'd be nuts to walk into your backyard where there has never been an apple seed planted and expect to pick apples off of an apple tree! Yet network marketers whine all the time about their businesses not growing, and they aren't planting any seeds! It's ludicrous!"

"I know I am totally guilty of that. I guess I get discouraged because people don't want to hear it or some people sign up and then quit or never do anything."

"A-ha," Tony exclaimed, "That's the sub-message of the passage I read you. There are four sub-messages. Let's look at them."

Tony read, "*As he was scattering the seed, some fell along the path, and the birds came and ate it up.*"

"*Some of the people you sow into will have the message stolen from them. The birds eat it. It might be their attitudes or the fact that someone told them it was a pyramid scheme or anything. The seed hits the ground, and the birds eat it. Nothing grows. And that's okay.*"

"*It is?*" Keller asked, somewhat surprised.

"*Of course, all part of life. Listen to the second one.*

Some fell on rocky places, where it did not have much soil. It sprang up quickly because the soil was shallow. But when the sun came up, the plants were scorched, and they withered because they had no root."

"*These are the people who get all excited and they jump right in. They run around with all their activity and then they just fizzle. It didn't go the way they wanted it to go or didn't go as fast as they expected and they quit. They had no root.*"

"*That sounds like my best friend, Mark. He quit.*"

"*And how much money will Mark make in your business? Nothing. Here's the third.*"

"*Other seed fell among thorns, which grew up and choked the plants.*

These are the people who get into the business, they might even do well, but then the worries of life choke them out. They forget to keep up on their business. They get distracted. They worry about money or what other people may think. Anything, really. And they get choked out. They die, and they never make it. Frankly, unless you get going, that would probably be you. You need to get moving!"

"I know. I really do. But I have to say; this is sort of depressing. So far you only told me about the people who don't make it. Do most people not make it?"

"Correct, most people don't make it. Sad, but that's okay."

"It's okay?"

"Of course! I make multiple millions of dollars a year; my top year was 8 million bucks, and most people in my team who signed up had quit. But I sowed enough seed that there were enough who stayed and it made me a fortune. It made a lot of other people fortunes too. And countless people an income that got the out of the rat race. Listen to the last kind of ground."

"Still other seed fell on good soil, where it produced a crop - a hundred, sixty or thirty times what was sown.

This is the seed that produces! These people are good seed who fall on good soil and listen - 30, 60, 100 times they produced over what was sown! AMAZING! Now, you don't know when you are talking to people what kind of ground they are. You just throw out the seed. What happens, happens."

"It all makes sense when you put it that way."

"I didn't put it that way. It's ancient wisdom, rooted in every aspect of life. You reap what you sow. Say it; I reap what I sow."

Keller felt weird, but he said it anyway, "I reap what I sow."

Tony stood up. "Look, man, that's the first law, and now I gotta jump. Don't worry about anything but sowing the seed. That's the only way you get to reap. Some will last and most won't, but the people who do will build a large business for you. Here's the test on whether you get the second law or not. Call me in a week if you have talked to at least 20 people. If you haven't, don't bother. You're a good kid with some real potential, but you have to prove yourself to me to warrant me spending more time with you. Let me see how you sow."

Keller stood up and shook Tony's hand. "Thank you. I definitely will. I promise."

"Talk is cheap. Just get it done. You'll be glad you did. Talk to you next week." With that, Tony jetted out the front door of Starbucks into the Arizona sun.

THE LAW OF ATTRACTION

On the eighth day, after their last meeting, Keller knew it was time to call Tony again. He was hoping that Tony hadn't changed his mind. As he sat in his sparsely furnished apartment, Keller punched in Tony's number into his cell phone and anxiously waited as it rang. He got voice mail. "*Hey Tony, it's Keller. I'm ready for my next lesson. Give me a call when you can.*" He pressed end and hoped he'd get a return call.

Not five minutes later his phone rang. The caller ID identified it as Tony. "*Hello?*"

"*Keller! What's happening, my friend?*"

"*Well, actually a lot. I'd like to take you up on your offer to get together again.*"

"*Did you talk to 20 people?*"

"*I've spoken to 24 people. Thought I'd over-deliver.*"

"*Perfect. What are you doing right now?*"

"*Just sitting here hanging, why?*"

"*Text me your address; I'll take you to lunch. Be ready to go in five minutes.*"

Keller was excited. "*Okay, I can do that. I'll be ready.*"

"*Lunch. See you soon.*" With that, Tony hung up, but Keller could hear that before he even hung up, Tony had already turned on his stereo and the music was blaring. Funny guy.

Seven minutes later, Tony pulled up to Keller's apartment building and honked the horn. Keller was just coming down the stairs when he noticed the car Tony was driving. *Whoa. What a beautiful car.*

When he reached the car, a 2014 Rolls Royce Phantom, he climbed in and buckled up. "*What a beautiful car.*"

"*Oh, this old thing?*" Tony said jokingly with a big grin on his face.

"*It's amazing. I'm a big car buff. This car is incredible.*"

"*Thanks, man. The seven laws gave me this car. Learned 'em, applied 'em, reaped the bounty. You will too.*"

"*I hope so. Where are we going for lunch?*

"*Oh, one of my favorite little spots. Over near my penthouse. Olive and Ivy. You know it?*"

"*Yeah, sure. I've eaten there before. It's great.*"

"*Perfect.*" Tony steered the $400,000 car out of the lot and headed to the restaurant.

When they got there, they were seated by a young woman who looked to be about 25. "*You have a girlfriend, Keller?*" Tony asked.

"*No, too busy.*"

"*You should get her number,*" Tony said, nodding toward the young woman who had seated them.

Keller blushed. "*Nah, I'm more interested in building my business right now. I like being single. And I'm here to learn the business from you.*"

"*That's my boy! I was just testing you. Wanted to see if you would get distracted.*"

The waitress came and offered them drinks. Keller had a Diet Coke, and Tony had an Arnold Palmer.

While they waited for their drinks to come, Tony asked, "*So, Heavy Hitter, tell me about your week. 24 people huh? That's good.*"

"*That's the most people I've talked to in a week.*"

"*So tell me how it went,*" Tony inquired.

The waitress interrupted them with their drinks. "*Can I take your order?*"

"*I know what I want,*" Tony said.

"*Go ahead and order,*" Keller said. "*I'll take a quick look.*"

"*Okay, I'll take the Lamb Gyro.*"

"*Great,*" the waitress said. "*And for you?*" she asked, looking at Keller. He was quickly scanning the menu.

"*I'll take the Chicken Panini.*"

"*Anything else?*" she asked

"*I think that's it,*" Tony confirmed.

After she had turned and walked away, Tony got down to business. "*24 people. Tell me about it. What happened with them. Give me an overview of the numbers. Sign-ups, customers, business builders, etc.*"

"*Okay, sure.*" Keller had memorized all the information because he figured Tony would want the breakdown. "*Here're the numbers: I talked to 24 people, made ten presentations, got two customers and two business partners.*" Keller couldn't hide that he was proud. It was the best week of his short network marketing career.

Tony held up his hand for a high-five, which Keller gladly accepted. "*That's incredible!*" Tony exclaimed. "*Awesome!*" Keller felt proud of himself. He was so thankful for meeting Tony and having him push him to the simplest of tasks: Just talk to people - Sow the seed. As they continued waiting, Keller filled Tony in on all the details of the meetings and the people who had signed up.

After their server had placed their food in front of them, Tony decided it was time for them to cover the second law. "*Are you ready for the second law?*"

"*Yes, of course!*"

"*Good. I call this the law of attraction. But it isn't the same as what has become popular lately. You could also call it the law of likability or even the law of positive attitude. Basically, it's this; People do business with people they are attracted to. It isn't what people typically think of with the modern concept of the law of attraction in that you just 'tell the universe what you want and it gives it to you.' I mean that we need to make ourselves attractive to other people.*"

Keller was a bit confused. "*You mean physically attractive?*"

"*No, although being physically attractive doesn't hurt, it's bigger than that. It means the customer is attracted to who you are and what you are doing. It intrigues them and moves them toward you. They can't stay away from you because they like you and what you stand for. They like where you are going. They want to be what you are, do what you do, and have what you have. So, it could be physical, but it includes who you are emotionally, spiritually, intellectually, relationally and of course, financially. What they see in you, they are attracted to.*"

During Tony's little speech, Keller was taking stock of himself internally and then responded, "*Well, what if you aren't that attractive, as you put it? I mean, I'm young, I don't have much experience, I'm pretty much broke, and I'm wondering what people would be attracted to when they look at me.*"

"*That's a fair point, Keller. I admit, it is much easier for me to recruit when I show up in a Rolls than when I pulled up in my ten-year-old Camaro.*" Keller chuckled. "*Success begets success. Yes, recruiting is easier when you are successful, but you have to start where you are. You will attract people who want what you want and what you are going for. There are always people worse off than you. And you can always bring in your successful upline to meet people and your potential prospects will be attracted to them, and subsequently, attracted to yourself. You can 'borrow their influence' so to speak.*"

"*I get it. My upline is cool. Good looking, well-educated and has a big business.*"

"*Perfect, but you can't always rely on that. You have to become someone who attracts people yourself.*"

"*Okay, I get it. But how do I do that?*"

"*Well, it's constant commitment to self-awareness and self-improvement. All those areas I just listed? Improve on them. Become excellent. Excellence attracts people. Why do you think companies hire famous athletes, actors, and performers to endorse their products? It ties them to excellence. And here's the key: YOU are the product! People are buying YOU. They are attracted to YOU. If they aren't attracted to you, if you aren't magnetic, then they'll pass on your opportunity.*"

"*Okay,*" Keller said as he finished his meal, "*Any specific things I should focus on?*"

"*Yes actually. Three things. First, positive people attract others. Be positive. Be the light. I don't mean that we should ignore negative circumstances, but we should overcome them and not let them affect our attitudes. The world beats people down, and positive people show them how to overcome it. Read positive books, listen to positive audios and music, think positive thoughts, speak positively and have a positive outlook on life. Always try and be optimistic in every situation. That will attract people to you. You will become a magnet for people. Yes, you will run across naysayers, but they are the wrong kind of people. You don't want them; You want individuals who want to be positive and maybe just haven't figured it out yet. They want a positive leader - you - and to engage in a positive culture - your company.*"

"*So are you always positive?*"

"*Oh, I have my down days. I'm human. But I've trained myself to focus and refocus on the positive. When I catch myself thinking negative thoughts, I make a choice to switch back to thinking positively. And here is a key: Listen to yourself talk. Take a week and listen to what you say. Your words tell the state of your attitude. What are you saying and how are you saying it?*"

"*I think I'm pretty good at that. My parents were very positive people, and I was raised that way. It's in my nature.*"

"*That's great, but get better; you can always be better. People who are continually getting better are attractive to other people. Here's the second key: Be visionary. Know where you are going and be able to articulate it.*" Tony paused. "*Tell me, Keller, where are you going? What's your vision?*"

"*That's a good question. I'm kind of floundering right now.*"

"*Bad answer. You think a person is attracted to someone who doesn't know where they're going?*"

Keller looked dejected.

Tony continued. "*Hey, I'm not trying to bust your chops or dishearten you. I'm just telling you that if you want to be successful and attract others, you have to have a crystal clear vision of your life. Your personal life and your business life. When someone says, 'Where are you going?' you have to be able to answer in a compelling way. You need to get a vision for your life. So my assignment for next time we meet is for you to have a compelling, specific vision for your life and business. And it needs to be inspiring! Nothing half-hearted, small or uninteresting.*"

"*Got it. I can do that. I will do that!*"

"*Awesome. Now here's the last thing to work on - and it is a work in progress; be successful. Success means being better tomorrow than you are today. Remember, success attracts. The more successful you become, the more people you will attract and the higher quality of people you will attract. Think about it. When you want advice on something, who do you seek out for that advice?*"

"*I guess the answer is successful people?*" Keller said more as a question than anything else.

"*Absolutely. Successful people. If you want to lose weight you ask the fit person, not the fat person. If you want to improve your marriage, you don't ask the couple who bickers all the time; you ask the couple who has been happily married for 40 years. When you want financial advice, you don't go to the guy standing on the side of the road with a cardboard sign in his hand; you ask for advice from someone who is rich. It's simple. People are attracted to successful people, so be successful."*

"*Okay, so that sounds easy, but how do you just be successful?*"

"*First, you start where you are. How much money do you make per year?*"

"*$30,000 about.*"

"*Yikes. How do you live on that?*" Tony asked with a smile on his face.

Keller smiled too. "*I know, right.?*"

"*But that's okay,*" Tony continued. "*Next year, make $60,000. Then the people who only make $40,000 will be attracted to you. They won't be attracted to someone who's making $30,000. Someone making $250,000 a year will only be attracted to someone making more. How many people in your networking business right now? Your downline.*"

"*About 15.*"

"*Alright, that's a start. Get it to 50, then 150, then 500. Be successful. The answer to all your problems is*" *to be successful. Go to the next level. Take your game up a notch, then another. Success has many levels. Just make sure you are always going up the ladder of success. When you are, you will take people with you.*"

The waitress had set the bill down on the table. Tony quickly grabbed it and paid it with cash, leaving a hefty tip. "*When you get successful, Keller, I expect you to buy me lunch!*" He laughed.

"*Gladly, Tony. You don't know how much this means to me.*"

"*My pleasure. Now let's get out of here, get you home, and get you back working the phones. You have prospects to get with!*"

"*Let's do it. Thanks for lunch.*"

As they were walking back to Tony's car, they noticed a man standing next to it, admiring the beautiful automobile.

"*Is this your car?*" the man asked.

"*It is,*" Tony replied. "*You like it?*"

"*Like it? I love it! It's got WOW written all over it.*" He paused for a moment then asked, "*Do you mind me asking what you do for a living that you can afford a car like this?*"

"*Not at all. I'm in network marketing.*"

"*You mean the 'you get two people who get two people who get two people' thing?*"

"*Well, that's one way of putting it. You want a car like this?*"

"*Man, that would be my dream.*"

Tony set the hook. "*I can help you make that happen. Let me give you my number. You can call me, we'll go to lunch, and I'll see if you're a fit for what I'm doing. Deal?*"

"*Deal!*" The man took Tony's number, and Tony and Keller jumped in the car to go.

"*See? Success attracts. Easy.*" He flashed Keller that Tony Maxwell smile and fired up the Rolls.

When Tony pulled into the parking lot, he said, "*I'll call you in a week or so. Get your vision for your life and business crystal clear. Make it big and make it detailed. That's the homework.*"

"*Will do, Tony. Thanks again!*"

THE LAW OF DISCIPLINE

It had been a few weeks since Tony and Keller had gotten together. Tony had been in six cities around the U.S., holding meetings for his teams. They had thousands of people at each event, all excited about their future in their business. When Tony got home, he gave himself a day to decompress from the travel and then decided to call Keller.

"*Hello?*" Keller answered.

"*Keller!*" he said excitedly. That was one of the many things people loved about Tony; he's always filled with excitement. A regular ol' Mr. Enthusiasm.

"*Tony, how are you?*"

"*Incredible, my friend. How are you?*"

"*Plugging away. Got sidetracked a little, but back at it.*"

"*Sidetracked?*" Tony questioned.

"*Yeah, I was pretty sporadic the last few weeks.*" He wondered if that would disappoint Tony.

"*Alright, buddy, time to get together again. If I have to, I'm going to pull you kicking and screaming into success,*" Tony said with a chuckle. "*What's your day look like?*"

"*After three, I'm wide open.*"

"*Done. I'll see you at 3:30. Come to my place. I'll text you the address. You can check in with the front desk, and they'll let you up. Oh, and bring your swimsuit. Maybe we'll take a dip in the pool.*"

"*Sounds like a deal, Tony.*"

"*Good. See you then.*"

Precisely at 3:30, Keller walked into the lobby of the most beautiful luxury condo complex in Scottsdale. Tony had called down to the desk ahead of time to let the guard know Keller was coming, so when he arrived the security guard waved him through.

When he got to the penthouse suite, Keller knocked on the door. Tony welcomed him in and gave him a brief tour of his 3500 square foot penthouse unit and then ushered him out to the back patio overlooking Scottsdale.

"*This place is beautiful,*" Keller said.

"*I know, I love it. It's amazing. I used to have a big mansion about twenty minutes from here, but I like the hustle and bustle of living downtown. All the restaurants and stores are just outside my door. I love the feel of living here.*" He waved his hand out at the valley. "*And you can't beat the view.*"

"*I'll say.*"

Tony got right down to business. "*So you got sidetracked.*"

"*Yeah, I didn't pick up my phone for a week because I had other things to do.*"

"*So how many people would you say you talked to over the last two weeks?*" Tony inquired.

"*Not many. Maybe eight or nine.*"

"*Okay then, time for law three. The law of discipline.*"

"*Discipline?*"

"*Yeah, I know, it isn't very sexy. I wish we had magic unicorns flying around spreading pixie dust that made everyone successful, but real success is pretty boring. The only way to get to a spectacular vision is through the tunnel of the mundane. Day in, day out, week in, week out, month in, month out, year in, year out. Discipline.*"

"*I need more discipline.*" Keller conceded.

"You know, there is an old quote of Jim Rohn's that says that 'Everyone must experience one of two pains, the pain of discipline or the pain of regret.'"

"Two pains?"

"Yeah, discipline is painful. At the very least it isn't as fun as non-discipline. It's more fun to eat ice cream on the couch than it is to go hit the gym, right?"

"For sure."

"It's more fun to spend your money than to save and invest it, right?"

"Definitely."

"So discipline is a pain. But it produces the joy of success."

"So what is the relation to regret? You said the pain of regret, right?"

"Yeah, so you have to choose one or the other, discipline or regret. But the difference, Jim Rohn said, was that discipline weighs ounces while regret weighs tons."

"Wow, profound."

"Right. Very profound. How many millions of people don't discipline themselves and let time pass by until they have no time left and then all they have left is regret?"

"Probably tens of millions. Or hundreds of millions."

"*Here's the key. It doesn't matter what you are talking about; success always comes through discipline. The baseball players who make it to the major leagues are the ones who disciplined themselves to take countless thousands of hours of batting practice growing up. You don't just walk onto a baseball field and swat a 95 mile an hour pitch into the grandstands. That comes from discipline. Successful investors become successful by studying the market daily for years. Their discipline allows them to make wise decisions based on the experience of their discipline. The people who are in excellent physical condition are the ones who discipline themselves every day to eat right and exercise their bodies. You don't get into great shape by only eating right and exercising once in a while.*"

"*I get that. Makes sense.*"

"*So for you, Keller, for all network marketers, it comes down to discipline. Will you be disciplined? Discipline happens because you make it happen. You aren't a victim of your circumstances. You decide what your circumstances are.*"

"*So, what are the things I need to be disciplined in to be successful at network marketing?*"

"*Good question. I've already mentioned the first two laws, sowing so you can reap and keeping a great attitude so you are attractive to others. But also, making presentations. I have a friend who I asked once what she would do if her company took away her multi-million dollars a year network marketing business and she had to start over. You know what she said? 'I'd fill my calendar with presentations.' Discipline. Make presentations every day. And follow up. The old saying is that the fortune is in the follow-up. Absolutely. But that is a discipline. Make a presentation and then put it in your calendar to follow up and don't miss it! This business is about discipline. Each company has some people in it who are making millions, and they usually follow a system, so you don't have to reinvent the wheel. You just have to discipline yourself to follow the proven systems."*

Keller looked a little overwhelmed, Tony noticed.

"*I know, it isn't naturally fun,*" Tony said, "*but you make it fun, and it gets really fun when the checks start rolling in. What isn't fun is making a half-baked, undisciplined, effort for a year, then petering out and regretting that you never built your business. That's no fun at all.*"

Keller stared off at the horizon for a few moments, thinking about how to discipline himself. Tony broke the silence. "*So, did you bring your suit?*"

"*I sure did.*"

"Great, let's get changed and go up to the rooftop. I have time for a quick dip, a cold beer, and one more law to share."

"Awesome, I'll get changed. Where should I go?"

"Guest bedroom. Let's do it!"

THE LAW OF MOMENTUM

Keller and Tony opened the doors to the rooftop pool and walked into the warm sunlight. "*Let's grab these two chairs right here in the sun,*" Tony said. "*Gotta work on my tan.*"

"*Sounds good.*" They set their beers on the table, and as soon as the bottom of Tony's can hit the table, he spun around and leaped into the pool. When his head broke the surface of the water, he exclaimed, "*This feels so good!*"

Keller stripped his shirt off and jumped in as well. "*The temp is just perfect.*"

"*Sure is. Nothing but the best at Tony's penthouse, baby!*"

Tony and Keller relaxed in the pool for ten or fifteen minutes before Tony suggested they drink their beer before it warmed up too much. "*Nothing worse than warm beer.*"

The two dried off and sat in the direct sunlight. "*I spent a majority of my formative years in Wisconsin, so I love the sun,*" Keller said.

"*I grew up in Seattle so I like real sunshine over liquid sunshine,*" Tony replied with a smile.

"*I get that.*" Keller laughed. He tipped his bottle to Tony. "*To the sunshine.*"

"*To the sunshine,*" Tony replied.

"*I know you said you have a teleconference in a little while, so how about that fourth law?*"

Tony took another sip of his beer. "*Ah yes, the fourth law. The law of momentum. I sometimes call it the hockey stick.*"

"*The hockey stick?*"

"*Yeah, I'll tell you why in a minute. First, what is momentum? Do you remember from school?*"

"*I know what momentum is, but I don't remember the equation.*"

"*It has to do with mass and velocity. The bigger the mass and the more velocity, the more momentum.*"

"*Makes sense, but how does that relate to network marketing?*"

"Simple. When you start out, there isn't much momentum. Your mass, the people on your team, is small. And your velocity isn't much either because your team doesn't grow very fast. Some people experience rapid growth, but that is the exception and not the rule. Most people who have long-term success build slow but sure, and they gain momentum over time. As their team becomes larger, say double in size, the team grows faster. That's momentum."

"Okay, I get it. But why is that one of the laws if not all people experience that?"

"I didn't say All, I said Most people don't experience that." Tony took another sip of his beer and adjusted his sunglasses. *"And most people don't give it enough time. They get discouraged about how slow it is going. Let me give you an example. Think of a train. You're getting ready for a cross-country trip on the train, and you just pull out of the station. You're a half mile into your trip, and you're only going five miles an hour. Imagine someone jumps up and says, 'This is going too slowly, we'll never get there. I'm getting off!' That'd be crazy, right? The train has a lot of mass, and it takes time to get it up to velocity. But ten miles out of the station, that train is at top speed. Thousands of tons of*

steel hurtling down the tracks at full speed. It has mega-momentum. It's very hard to stop!"

The light clicked for Keller. "*Most people quit before they gain their momentum.*"

"*That's it. I'll tell you about a guy who really blew it. He worked his business hard for about a year and had about 1600 people in his business. Then he got mad at the owner of the company, went crazy, and left his business. He had already done all the work! He was on the cusp of momentum. He moved on to work for another company and had to start the whole thing over again, wasted a year of his life. It happens all the time. You want to ride the momentum, not quit or get sidetracked when it hits or is about to hit! The real key is to understand the nature of momentum. It builds over time and becomes more and more unstoppable. Look, I have put hundreds of thousands of people into my business over the years, and my team is so big now that it just continues to grow. It has mass and velocity! I could never work another day for the rest of my life, and I'd still be making bank. It has broken away from me, basically having a life of its own. It would eventually slow down, of course, but the momentum is so huge that it would pretty much last a lifetime.*"

"*Wow. That's amazing. Hey, I remember you said something about a hockey stick. What does that mean? How does that relate to momentum?*"

"*Ah, yes. I use the term hockey stick because some financial guys say that some long-term investment charts look like a hockey stick lying on its side. Relatively flat and then all of the sudden it surges straight up - or nearly straight up. A lot of successful network marketing businesses look like that on paper. I knew a woman who worked her business for eight years. Her first checks were $25, $50 a month. They grew very slowly until year eight. Then they went like this: $500, $800, $1200, $1600, $2500, $3500 until she got to year nine where she was making $40,000 a month, residual income. How many people would work a business for eight years, with little return, even with a promise that they would make $40,000 a month forever? Hardly anyone. Successful people are patient enough for momentum to kick in.*"

"*Yeah, it would be hard to wait. It is always hard to be patient.*"

"*Success comes to the patient, the persistent, the diligent, for they shall reap momentum.*" Tony drank the last sip from his bottle. "*Most people quit before payday, and payday is when that velocity hits. Think about a young couple that starts investing $100 a month*" at 25 years old. After a year they would have $1200 plus some interest. Now would it be smart for them to say, 'We hardly made any money! We're going to stop saving for retirement!'"

"*Yeah, that wouldn't be smart at all,*" Keller said.

"*Of course not. Because over time, their investments double, the mass grows, and the velocity grows. If they have discipline, 40 years down the road, they could be making millions of dollars! Their investment would finally hit momentum - and their chart would look like a hockey stick!*"

At that moment Tony's phone rang. It was his admin. "*Uh-huh. Okay. Tell him I'll call him in fifteen minutes.*" Tony hung up and looked at Keller. "*Gotta go put a fire out. Let's get out of here.*"

After Keller had changed back into his clothes, Tony was ready to make his call.

"*That was great stuff, Tony. I'm going to be disciplined. I'll take money making actions every day. Over time, I'll hit momentum.*"

"*Thatta-boy! Go get 'em. I have to jump on this call. Let's talk next week. Bring me some good reports!*"

With that, Keller walked out the front door, newly inspired.

THE LAW OF MULTIPLICATION

After not seeing each other for a month, due to their dedication to their respective businesses, Tony decided it was time for Keller to learn the fifth law. He punched Keller's number into his cell phone and called him.

Keller's phone flashed "*Tony*" and he answered, "*Tony! How's it going?*"

"*Great,*" Tony responded. "*What are you doing Saturday?*"

"*Saturday? Nothing scheduled. Why?*"

"*I need to teach you the fifth law, the Law of Multiplication. Or sometimes, as I call it 'Are you smarter than a 3rd grader.'*"

"*What do you mean, 'Are you smarter than a 3rd grader?'*"

Tony didn't answer, instead of telling him he said, "*I'll tell you Saturday. I have a thousand people on my team coming to a meeting on Saturday from nine until five. At three, I'm teaching the fifth law. You can come for the whole meeting if you want but for sure be there at three. I'll text you the details.*"

"*Okay, I'll be there!*" Keller was excited. He had read on the internet how Tony was a dynamic speaker and he couldn't wait to hear him in person, speaking to a large crowd.

Saturday, around 2:30 in the afternoon, Keller approached the registration table in the foyer of the hotel's large ballroom. He could hear an energetic crowd inside the room behind the table. He spoke to the middle-aged man at the table. "*Hi, my name is Keller, and I was invited by Tony Maxwell to hear him speak at three.*"

"*Yes, Keller, I've been expecting you. Tony told me to be on the lookout for your arrival. Come with me, and I'll take you to the green room.*"

They walked along the outside of the ballroom until they reached the back. The man knocked on the door, waited until it was open, then he and Keller went inside. Keller could immediately see Tony back by the rear projection machine. Tony saw Keller as well.

"*Keller, great to see you!*" He motioned for Keller to take a seat on a chair set up in a group of furniture that looked like a living room. There was a whole buffet with an assortment of drinks there as well. "*Grab yourself something to drink and eat. I'll be there in a minute.*"

While Tony finished his conversation, Keller grabbed a few bacon-wrapped dates and a Diet Coke and sat down. Moments later, Tony joined him and seated himself on the couch next to Keller's chair.

"*Glad you made it, man!*"

"*Me too. I'm excited to see you speak.*"

"*Well, I go on soon, but we can chat a bit beforehand. How is it going?*"

"*It's going well. I've grown my team to 34 people in the last two months, and they're the right people. They are all working and building their teams. I'm happy with how it's going and I give you most of the credit.*"

"*Well, my friend, give yourself credit. You wouldn't believe how many people I've taught these laws to who don't apply them. Your business is growing because you are using the lessons you've learned.*

"*I don't know how someone could learn these and see what you have created for yourself and not apply them.*"

"*Oh you know, you can lead a horse to water, but you can't force it to drink, right?*"

"*I guess, but it seems stupid.*"

"*It is stupid. Someone hands you a golden ticket, and you never redeem it? Stupid.*"

Keller caught Tony up on all the activity of his team over the last few months, the ups and downs, and how it is growing. As he was talking, a young woman approached Tony and said, "*Mr. Maxwell, 5 minutes until you go on.*"

Tony thanked the woman and then said to Keller, "*Mr. Maxwell. I feel uncomfortable being called Mr. Maxwell. I'm Tony! My dad is Mr. Maxwell. Anyways, listen, I'm doing a short training in a few minutes on the fifth law - I've done some of the others today as well - but I want to give you a preview. The fifth law is the law of multiplication.*"

Keller interjected, "*Otherwise known as 'Are you smarter than a 3rd grader?'*"

Tony laughed. "*Exactly. If you are smarter than a 3rd grader, you can make a fortune in this business! Look, the people who get successful in this business understand people and sales, but they also have to have a basic understanding of math. Multiplication to be precise. The money is in the math - the right kind of math.*"

"*The right kind? What do you mean?*"

Right at that moment, the introduction for Tony's stage appearance started, and he jumped up. "*Gotta run. There is a seat in the front row with a sheet that has your name on it. Go grab your seat - and take notes!*" Tony flashed that famous Tony Maxwell smile and moved toward the steps behind the stage.

Keller got to his seat just as the announcer said: "*And now, ladies and gentlemen, put your hands together for one of the legends of our industry, your team leader, Toooooooony Maaaaaxwell!*"

The crowd of nearly 1100 people went out of their minds crazy. The sound system was blaring AC/DC's Thunderstruck as Tony came out to speak to his adoring fans. After nearly a two-minute standing ovation, Tony got the crowd to calm down and sit in their seats.

"*Hey guys, you all look amaaazing!*" The crowd cheered again. "*Are you ready to rock this place and learn a simple lesson that will explode your business?*" Again, ear-shattering applause and cheering.

Tony moved to the front of the stage. "*I have a question. How many of you are smarter than a 3rd grader?*" Nearly everyone's hand went up in the air. "*Now I see a lot of hands going up, but I gotta tell you, I don't know that you are because the average 3rd grader learns something that almost no network marketers get, or at least they don't apply it.*

"*I'm talking about the fifth of my seven laws of network marketing - the law of multiplication.*" Tony moved right as a camera moved toward him and beamed his image up on the overhead screens. "*In first grade, you learn addition. That's the simple stuff. One plus one equals two. Two plus two equals four. That's basic math. First graders know that. Most network marketers understand addition.*"

Tony quieted his voice. "*Ah, but 3rd graders... 3rd graders learn something more powerful. It's like addition on steroids. And for the network marketers who get smarter than a 3rd grader, this is explosive! What is the secret? The law of multiplication.*

"*Addition is simple. Multiplication is more complicated but gets you to much bigger numbers. Four plus four is eight but four times four is sixteen! Ten plus ten is twenty but ten times ten is one hundred! Fifty plus fifty is one hundred but fifty times fifty is twenty-five hundred!*

"Here is the math as it relates to the money: Addition will make you an income, but multiplication will make you a fortune!

"Addition is selling. Addition is your direct customers. Let's say you make $15 a month off of your direct customer's purchases. Let's say you have 20 customers. That's $300 a month in income. Not bad. That's a car payment for a decent car. And let's say you add another 20 customers. That's now 40 customers. And you add another $300. That's okay; that would pay for a nice little vacation once a year. But you aren't going to get wealthy with addition. You could add another 60 customers in the next year, busting your tail to do it, and you get yourself to 100 customers. What is that? $1500 a month. That's okay. That's fine. But it wouldn't get most of you out of your day job. And it certainly won't give you financial security.

"Now let's talk about multiplication. Addition is selling, but multiplication is building! Let's start again with those 20 people. You spend your time helping them build their own business. Those 20 people each go out and get 20 people in their businesses. What do you have now? 400 people who you earn money from. Would you like the money from 400 people? Of course you would. Now here is where it gets crazy. You teach those 400

people to build a team of 20 people. Now, what do you have? Eight thousand people! Who wants the income of eight thousand people?" The crowd again went wild.

"*Friends, it's simple math. Start with addition, of course, but then get smarter than a 3rd grader and do the multiplication!*" Tony moved to the center of the stage. "*Now, because I am not just about theory, but about practical advice, we are going to practice our multiplication right here, right now. Here is what we are going to do. There are at least 1000 people here today. Let's call it 1000. I am going to give you thirty minutes where all you are going to do is call people right there from your seat and book personal presentation meetings for the next week. We call them PPM's. Pull out your cell phones, go through your contact list and dial for dollars, baby. Just get them to agree to sit down with you in the next week. I know that earlier you heard how to ask for the PPM so now is your time to practice. In thirty minutes we should be able to average three PPms per person. Some of you will get less and some more, but let's set a goal of 3000 PPM's booked in the next half hour. Are you ready?*"

The crowd went wild again and they began to cheer, "*Rea-dy, Rea-dy, Rea-dy!*" Tony smiled.

"*Okay, the guys are going to put a countdown clock on the overhead screen. Ready, set, GO!*"

The people pulled out their cell phones and started dialing. Math at work.

Exactly 30 minutes later, Tony took the stage again. "*Alright everyone, put down your cell phones. Let's get a count.*" The staff handed out report sheets, and when they were all turned in and tabulated, Tony came back on stage, right after another speaker gave a short motivational speech. "*Alright gang, here it is, the moment to reveal the numbers. Are you ready?*" The crowd roared enthusiastically. "*The total amount of PPM's booked out of this room in the last half hour is... 3467!*"

The entire crowd jumped to its feet, cheering. Tony calmed them down and had them take their seats. "*Okay, and now I have a special reward. I am going to give $5000 CASH MONEY to the person who reported the most PPM's booked in the last half hour. Is that awesome or what? Okay, this person booked NINE PPM's in a half hour! That's like one every three and a half minutes! Let's bring her up, Janet Lewis!*" The crowd went crazy. They loved it. When she got up on stage, Tony counted out 50 one-hundred dollar bills into Janet's hand. The crowd counted along. One hundred, two hundred, three hundred... They kept going until he had handed her all $5000.

After giving Janet her prize, Tony began wrapping up his time on stage. "*Folks, we have one more speaker here in just a minute, but let me close with this. It is all about the math. Remember: Addition will make you an income, but multiplication will make you a fortune!*" Tony waved to the crowd and made his exit to the back of the stage as music blared overhead.

Keller got up from his seat and met Tony in the back. "*Awesome job, Tony.*"

"*Thanks, man. It is always fun talking to a group that big in a room full of energy.*"

"*I can imagine. Say, can we grab dinner after the event?*"

"*Oh, I wish I could, but I'm totally booked. I've been thinking, though, I have a boat on Lake Pleasant and wondering if you want to come waterskiing with me next weekend? It'll be fun.*"

"*Sure, that would be incredible. You'll get me the details next week?*"

"*Yep, for sure. Listen, I'm packed here for the rest of the afternoon and evening. Gotta run. Thanks for coming. Practice your multiplication. I'll get with you next week.*"

They shook hands and Keller headed to his car. He thought again about Tony's words; *Addition will make you an income, but multiplication will make you a fortune!*

THE LAW OF LEADERSHIP AND SALES

L ake Pleasant was beautiful that Saturday afternoon, 79 degrees and not a cloud in the sky. Tony had invited a few of his top leaders from his organization in addition to Keller for a day of waterskiing on the lake, sunbathing and a few cold beverages. Tony's boat was a 36-foot cigarette racer, fast and perfect for pulling a skier. He even had an extravagant tube that held three people that he used to tow his friends who didn't waterski. Tony, while enjoying the fruit of his wealth, enjoyed sharing that wealth with his family, friends and business associates even more. And not much made him happier than being on the lake in the sunshine with his friends in his spectacular speedboat.

After a full day of boating, Tony and his friends went to one of the local restaurants where they had burgers, wings, and beer. They talked endlessly about the excitement they felt about their business and how technology had enabled them to grow their businesses exponentially. Keller was in awe. He knew leaders in his company who were successful, but he hadn't ever been able to get close to them like he was with Tony's top leaders tonight. Most of his knowledge about these people came through the company magazines, the website, and from seeing them from afar on the stage at the national events the company put on twice a year.

As they had an after-dinner drink, Tony brought up the sixth law. "*Keller, these guys have all heard the sixth law, but I wanted to share it with you, with my friends here, because they have all used this law to grow their businesses to where they are making at least $40,000 a month.*"

"*Cool,*" Keller said. "*I'm all ears!*"

"*Okay, so the sixth law I call the law of leadership and sales. Let me ask you, Keller, which of these is more important in building a network marketing business?*"

"*Easy. Definitely sales,*" Keller replied confidently.

Tony smiled. "*Ah, not so easy. The answer is leadership.*"

"*Leadership? Network marketing is sales. Some people even call it direct selling now.*"

"*True. There are sales involved, but selling isn't what will build you a huge business with an incredible, long-term, residual income. Leadership skills will do that.*"

"*How so? How do I use leadership skills when I'm out selling a product?*"

"*Let me be clear; sales skills are crucial. You ought to become the best salesman that you can be, for sure. But leadership skills will be what build a large organization.*" Tony pointed to his friend Matt, who was sitting two to the right of Keller. "*Matt makes $125,000 a month. Matt, let me ask you a question. What percentage of your time is spent working on your business now versus working on other people's businesses?*"

"*Right now I spend about 10% of my time on my own business versus 90% of my time helping others build their businesses,*" Matt answered.

"*So you are doing more leading than selling, right?*" Tony asked.

"*Absolutely. But it wasn't always that way. When I started out it was almost the opposite. 90-10 for selling.*"

"*So how - or when - do you switch?*" Keller asked.

"*It's gradual,*" Tony said. "*When you are starting out, there is no one to lead. You have to sell. And the better you sell, the more customers you pick up. And you sell to prospective business builders. Of course, some of your customers will also become business builders. You start out by mastering selling. Read all the books, go to the seminars, listen to the audios, learn everything you can about selling and get very, very good at it. You will build out a nice little customer base, pick up some business builders and grow your downline. That comes from selling. But as your team grows, you need to be helping them improve their teams. I've seen people build a six-figure a month income with less than twenty personal customers and less than twenty direct business builders.*"

"*Wow. Well, I guess when you put it that way, it makes sense,*" Keller said.

"*You know what it's like?*" Tony asked Keller.

"*What?*"

"*Addition and multiplication. Sales skills will add, and leadership skills will multiply. Sales skills will build an income, while leadership skills will make a fortune. So when you start, you're selling, but as your team grows, you start to slide the percentage over to become more of a leader, helping others build their business. Now, even when you get a significant residual income,*" you still have to work on your business, but that isn't where the money comes from. When you sell ten more people your products, you make $150. When you help ten of your downline build a team of 100 people each, you create another 1000 people you make money off of from their volume."

"*So how do you become a better leader?*" Keller asked.

Tony nodded at Meagan, a younger woman of about thirty-five, who had a large business. "*Meagan, you are one of the best leaders I know. What would you say are the keys to becoming a better leader?*"

Meagan put her drink down before she answered. "*Good question. I didn't start out as a good leader. I had never actually led anything in my whole life. I had done a little selling but wasn't even really good at that. But Tony taught me the importance of learning leadership. So I consumed every type of media about leadership that I could get my hands on; I read every single book I could find on the topic, went to seminars on leadership, took copious notes, watched everything I could online and then I put these things into practice. I learned through trial and error. Sometimes I failed, but most of the time I succeeded. In the end, I built a great team, and it was all built on leadership.*"

Tony chimed in. "*When was the last time you studied leadership, Keller?*"

"*I can't even remember. I think I had to read a leadership book when I was in student government in high school, but I don't even remember what it was really about.*"

"*Well, here's your challenge: Start reading two leadership books a month for the next year, go to at least one leadership conference in the next year, and watch at least one video a week on leadership. Then as you learn and as you see how the things you are learning are pertinent to your business, apply the information.*"

"*I can do that,*" Keller replied.

"*You have to do that!*" Tony said. "*Your success depends on it.*"

After teaching the sixth law, everybody had one more drink before Tony picked up the check. The friends hugged each other goodbye and went on their way. Tony pulled Keller aside in the parking lot. "*One more law to learn, right? How do you think they are going so far?*"

"*Incredible, Tony. I can't wait to get the last one.*"

"*Well, I want to find just the right time to teach you the last one. It may be the most important, so I want to make sure you remember it. I'll be in touch with you.*"

"*Sounds like a deal. I'll be waiting - and working.*"

THE LAW OF CHOICE

Tony wanted to make a real impact on Keller for the last lesson, so he invited him to go on a sightseeing flight on his new jet to Las Vegas and back. Round trip would only be a couple of hours tops. Tony had recently taken ownership of a Cessna Citation M2, a small, six-passenger business jet. One of the best things about being rich was Tony didn't have to fly commercial anymore. He sometimes did, but anytime he could use his jet, he did. He often had lunch and even champagne in the jet for the tour.

Keller was as excited as a kid in a candy shop. Tony's cars were extraordinary, and his boat was fantastic. The penthouse condo was extraordinary, but a jet? It blew Keller's mind. He parked at the Scottsdale airport and walked to the hangar. As he approached the hangar, the jet was already out and ready to fly. Tony was waiting at the bottom of the stairs, enjoying the Scottsdale sun.

"*You ready to fly?*" Tony asked Keller

"*Absolutely,*" Keller exclaimed.

"*Then let's do it!*" Tony turned and went up the stairs to the plane with Keller quickly following him. The cabin door closed, and soon the jet was cleared for takeoff. Keller loved the feeling of the thrust of jet engines. Commercial flying was fun to Keller, but this was beyond fun. The plane's wheels left the tarmac started its steep incline, giving Tony and Keller a full view of the area.

"*I thought we could eat lunch, talk, and take a quick trip up to see the Las Vegas skyline,*" Tony said.

"*Sounds great.*" Keller was eager to learn the last law.

The two talked about everything they had been doing since they last saw each other. Keller's team was now 125 people strong. The laws had worked, and he was excited to share his success with Tony. The last thing he would want would be to learn all these laws and fail. Having an opportunity to learn from one of the top income earners of all time and not apply it, and succeed at it, would be a travesty. But the laws worked.

Keller now believed they would work for anyone who would take them seriously and apply themselves.

About a half hour into the flight to Vegas, they broke out the boxed lunches Tony had catered and opened the champagne. *This is living.* Keller thought. Over their food, they talked about life, dreams and things they wanted to accomplish.

Soon they were doing a loop around the Vegas strip, checking out the iconic hotels and casinos. It was just as impressive during the day as at night, just not as shiny.

When they started back toward Phoenix, Keller decided to tell Tony something he had been thinking about. "*You know Tony; I don't understand why you stopped by my table that first day in Starbucks. And I don't see why you decided to take me under your wing and teach me how to do this business, but I'll be forever grateful that you did. You opened my eyes and changed my life. Thank you.*"

"*Keller, it is no problem at all. I'm just passing it on. You know, I didn't grow up rich. I didn't have many advantages. I was broke. I had maybe $100 to my name and a credit score in the low 400's. Then someone told me about network marketing, and I saw a way that I could achieve my dreams. I had nowhere to go but up!*

Fortunately, I had a great mentor. The billionaire founder of our company took a liking to me, as did one of the top income earners of all time. They helped me, and now I help others. That's the way it's supposed to be."

"Well, I'm glad you helped me."

"With their help, I became a top income earner myself, and now I can do whatever I want, whenever I want, all because of network marketing. It's extraordinary. Little time commitment and total financial freedom." Tony looked at his watch and realized they only had about 30 minutes left in the flight, so he decided to give Keller the seventh and final law. *"Are you ready for law number seven?"*

"More than ready," Keller said.

"Great. The seventh law is called the law of choice. Ultimately your life is your choice. Everything that you achieve or don't achieve is your choice. The money you make, how much you weigh, where you live, everything about your life is your choice."

"But don't you think there are some people that have no choice? People who can't change where they are at?"

"I don't. Well, maybe someone who lives in a hut in the jungle in Africa, or in rural China. They may be stuck there with limited choices, but I'm talking about the vast majority of people who live in the free world.

Those people are governed by choice, not by chance. The problem is that no one wants the responsibility that comes with knowing they are where they are because they chose to be there. Most people want to play the victim. They are controlled by their circumstances. They act as though they accidentally live where they live, work where they work and everything else they are disgruntled with."

"But what about poor people in small towns? Often they have no way out."

"That is a victim mentality. They can move. They don't have to stay in that small town. They can work and save everything they can and leave. They can change their life. Millions of people have done it. No one is ever stuck."

"I guess so," Keller said, becoming convinced.

"I know so," said Tony. *"It happened to me, and I've seen firsthand how people have chosen to work hard and live the life of their dreams. It is possible. But back to what I was saying, most people won't accept responsibility because they are afraid. They have nothing to be scared of, though.*

"If it's true that they are where they are because of their choices, then it's also true that wherever they want to be, or whatever they want to accomplish or achieve is

simply a matter of..." His voice trailed off, suggesting to Keller to finish the sentence.

"*Their future choices.*"

"*BINGO! Their future choices. If where they are now is based on past choices, then where they want to go is simply based on the choices they make from here on out. They just have to decide what they want and then make the decisions to get there.*"

"*That makes total sense,*" Keller agreed. "*I can see how my choices up to now have created the life I'm living.*"

"*And it works for better or for worse,*" Tony continued. Just then the pilot informed them that they were beginning the descent back to the Scottsdale airport. "*Bad choices produce bad results, average choices produce average results, and great choices produce great results! Sure, obstacles get thrown in your way from time to time, but that happens to everyone. Just keep making great choices.*"

"*So what do you think are the choices most successful people make, especially those in network marketing?*"

"*Good question. Let me think.*" After a moment, Tony began again. "*I would say there are things every successful network marketer chooses:*

- Choose to serve others. It isn't about you. It is about helping others.
- Choose to persist. There will be tough times. Winners don't quit.
- Choose to be disciplined. There will always be distractions. Stay focused every day.
- Choose to be a leader. Get out front, inspire and take risks.
- Choose to think big. It is just as easy to think big as it is to think small.
- Choose to be positive. Negative thinking will never help you succeed.
- Choose to stay until payday. Building a business takes time, but it pays off in the end.

"*That's what I think of off the top of my head. It is all about choices. And now you have a choice before you.*" As Tony said this, the wheels of the jet touched down. They would soon be back at the hangar. "*You are a young guy. You're smart. You have what it takes. You have the knowledge. Now you have a choice. You've learned the laws and you've started your journey with a team of over 100 people. You are on your way. But you will continue to make choices that will take you one way or the other. Every day you have choices and those choices determine your future.*

Keller sat in deep thought. *Choices.*

Tony slapped him on the knee. "*I have an excellent feeling about you. I did the first time I met you. You're going to do great. Just keep making great choices and let the results pile up.*"

The jet came to a standstill, and the door opened up.

"*I will, Tony. I promise I will.*"

"*And when you succeed, pay it forward. Help others. Take someone by the hand and lead them along.*"

"*I will for sure do that, just like you did for me.*"

Tony and Keller got off the plane and said their good-byes.

"*Thanks for the great flight. That was a trip of a lifetime. So cool.*"

"*No problem, my friend. It was fun.*"

"*So we're done with the laws. Now what?*" Keller wondered outloud.

"*Now you apply them and reap the reward.*"

"*So will I see you again? Can we stay in touch?*"

"*Of course, Keller! We're friends now.*" Tony stuck his hand out, and Keller met it with his hand.

"*Friends. That's cool,*" Keller said.

"*All right buddy, you know me, blowin' and goin'. I got another meeting.*" Tony went to the hangar while

Keller watched. Soon Tony pulled out in his new Lamborghini Aventador and headed for the exit. He rolled the window down and waved to Keller. Keller waved back.

Now I have to go and make MY dreams come true.

THE SEVEN LAWS OF NETWORK MARKETING VIDEO TRANSCRIPT

A s the seed idea for *The 7 Laws of Network Marketing*, here is a transcript of the video that Anthony and Chris produced to teach the Seven Laws of Network Marketing. Learn and Enjoy!

Chris Widener: Hi and welcome to the seven laws of network marketing.

Anthony Powell: My name is Anthony Powell.

Chris Widener: And I am Chris Widener. It is fortunate for us to be together because Anthony is one of the all-time income earners in this industry of network marketing and a multiple 7 figure earner.

Anthony Powell: And Chris is Wall Street Journal and New York Times best- selling author, having sold millions of books and spoken to millions of people around the world.

Chris Widener: And one of the things that are unique to Anthony and I is that we were both mentored by the legend Jim Rohn.

Together we're going to tell you the seven laws of network marketing. Anthony, the first law of network marketing success, is the law of sowing and reaping.

Anthony Powell: Yeah Chris, and you know sowing and reaping, a lot of people don't understand the power of sowing and reaping. First, you have to plant the seed. So what does that mean? You have to invite enough people to your presentations, and today people do presentations online and offline. But you have to do the numbers if you will. You have to plant enough seeds for you to reap a big enough crop.

Chris Widener: You know our mentor Jim Rohn he used to talk about the law of sowing and reaping as well, and it comes from the Bible. He would talk about how the sower would go out, and he would throw the seed. He threw the seed, and some of the seed landed on dry soil, and the birds ate it, and some of the seed landed on rocky soil, and some of the seed landed in thorns. But there was always the seed that landed on the good soil. Can you help us make that analogy for network marketing?

Anthony Powell: Think of it this way, you know when you invite people, or when you throw enough seeds out in the community, you are going to get somebody to show up to your meeting. But just because someone attends your meeting or goes through your sales funnel does not mean they are going to sign up. So what that means is you have to throw enough seeds out there meaning you've got to have enough invitations to have enough presentations.

The bottom line is the law of averages. You know, what you lack in skill you make up in numbers. Chris and I think that is what a lot of network marketers or affiliate marketers don't get. They want to reap; they want this big check, but they don't understand that this is a business, and for you to understand the business you have to learn how to sow.

I will tell you my little numbers if you don't mind. You know, for every three invites I make I will get one person who attends my presentation. For every three people that I present to, I will get one person signed up in my business or as a customer. And then as time progressed I got my numbers fine-tuned to where I could figure out how many people I had to get to sign up to get a leader.

See, the art of this business is not just about signing people up. The art is to get enough customers and get enough people to help you distribute. But you can't do that if you don't understand the definition of sowing, which is to invite, present and then the most important thing is launching people's businesses, ultimately allowing you to reap your crop, get you an opportunity to start to cash in.

It is a process, though, so you have to have that patience that we are going to talk about in a minute. When I started at 19 years old, Larry Thompson, Mark Hughes, and Jim Rohn introduced me to the industry, and they took me under their wing.

If you just do the numbers and you don't look up, and you do it day in and day out, we will teach you what the numbers are. Sooner or later your day is going to come. By doing just that I got down to signing up ten people a month. Out of ten people, I got two leaders. Those two leaders I drove and taught them what to do, but you see, I didn't get to the top with only one person signed up, Chris. I sowed, and it allowed me to reap, and after my first year, you're not going to believe what happened: $7000 a month by doing this sowing and reaping. I fired my boss. I had a firing my boss party, and more importantly by the age of 26 - I still can't believe it - the day I financially retired, all because someone taught me sowing and the reaping.

Chris Widener: Yeah I have heard that over and over again.

Anthony Powell: And some treat it like a hobby. Do you think Dell computers sells three laptops a month and says "Wahoo."? That's not what they do.

Chris Widener: They sell millions and millions and millions. They are getting out there, but they started in a little college dormitory. You know you talked about people that want the reaping without the sowing. Let's take that in its most literal sense. My dad's family was all from Nebraska. They are all farmers, right? Imagine if a farmer went out at reaping time and he says "There's nothing here. There are no crops here." Well did you sow the seed? Did you put the seed in the ground? You don't reap without sowing.

So let's talk about the 2nd law; the law of attraction that we also call the law of likeability and attitude. How important is the law of attraction and being liked and having a positive attitude in this business?

Anthony Powell: It starts with making a decision about where you want to go and who you want to be.

You have to search that out within yourself. I thought it was a trick because I thought "What do you mean I haven't got an attitude? You mean I just have to smile and get rich?" and everyone snickered and looked at me and said "No son, that is not the way it works."

See, what you have to understand is you have to attract people. One of the things my mentor, Mark Hughes, said, "Son, bring $20,000 a month to the phone even though you don't have it." You are going to attract people who want to go where you are going. People are going to feel that you are going with or without them, and if you do that, you are going to attract people who want to go with you. And that, my friends, is going to give you an opportunity to build something. You become likable, and we all want to be likable, but first you have to have the attitude. You have to know where you are going. You have to tell your mind that you are already there. Then you have to get up, day in and day out, and whether you like it or not, well... you are going to love it actually; you are going to attract people.

When I first got going, I essentially threw a dart on the wall; Next thing I know I'm moving to Houston, Texas. Can you believe that? I wanted to change my center of influence. I listened to Jim Rohn audios while I jogged 2 or 3 miles a day, and then I just got on the phone, and I did the sowing and reaping. And I changed. Believe it or not, I drove my check so fast because I was attracting people to go with me[

Chris Widener: Yes success always starts with the attitude and the mindset and you know there are lots of things that you will not be able to control. In the world you can't control the economy, you can't control the weather, and there are going to be lots of things that you can't control in your business. But the number one thing that you do have total control over is your attitude and your mindset. So it doesn't matter if things are going amazing or you have some hardships, successful people understand the law of attraction that comes from likeability and attitude. You set the course for your life by determining in your mindset, your attitude, what makes you inspirational to other people and attracts people, and people want to do business with people they like.

Chris Widener: Let's talk about law number three, the law of discipline. The law of discipline is not a very sexy law. I mean, I wish there were magic unicorns. I wish we could blow some magic pixie dust and make you successful, but this is where the rubber hits the road. The law of discipline, of consistency, of persistence; talk to us about how you built your massive business understanding that law of discipline.

Anthony Powell: This is probably the number one thing I have to tell everybody. I have been asked this question so many times, "How did you build your organization as big as you did?" I built one of the largest businesses in this industry of all time - hundreds of thousands of people several times over in my organization - and that just doesn't happen. But it happened because of discipline, consistency, and definitely persistence.

My mentor, the one that got me involved in my first business and where I built my first big group, he called and said, "Hey Anthony, do you remember when you were 19 and 20 years old? The day you pushed your car to start? Did you know it's 12 years later, and you're still doing the same thing, and you don't need to make money anymore? You see that's why you are making it so big. If people could just understand you're doing the same thing day in day out no matter what, you're doing it every day.

One of the things I learned from Jim Rohn is you have to be consistent at being consistent. We all want money, right? So we're all trying to make money. But the bottom line is you have to get up early, and you have to make additional calls. On your lunch break, you'll need to go out in the parking lot and do even more calls, do things to promote and build your business and then when you come home you have got to get focused again on the weekend.

You have to make deals with your family. Schedule time with your family that allows you to be present with them and have your life, but get yourself out of that linear income trap. If you want out of that trap, you're going to have to stay disciplined. You have to follow through. You have to be consistent. There is no secret to building a fortune. You read about how the rich got rich, and they worked from the bottom to the top.

These are the biggest rules: Discipline, consistency, persistence. Practice them over and over, but make sure you don't just do it. Learn your numbers. As Jim Rohn said, you might be two millimeters off. So if you are staying disciplined, the same two millimeters might be on the right track, there are your million dollars. Or you are two millimeters off, and you lose the million. I had to establish my work habits, I had to be smart, but I had to stay disciplined, and I have always outworked my team. I mean it is something that is important.

Chris Widener: A top income earner in her company invited me to speak at a big network marketing conference, and during my talk, in front of the entire audience, I asked her, "If your company came to you and said 'Once you hit the top income earner, we reset you. We take away your business and start you all over again.' What would you do?" Without even missing a beat - and she is a lady that has made 10 of millions of dollars - she says, "I would fill my calendar." That is what she said. "Everyday fill my schedule, show presentations, talk to people and put them in the business."

That is discipline, people who do it day in, day out, week in, week out. It doesn't matter if you are talking about network marketing or you are talking about becoming a professional athlete, people who succeed are people who day in day out are studying and working hard. Too many people get into network marketing, and they think it is going to be magic potion and they don't discipline themselves.

So let's talk about the fourth law, the law of momentum. You love this law because you talk about it all the time. Tell us about the law of momentum.

Anthony Powell: The hardest thing in business to get is momentum. If you are from the city, like me, you probably went to the zoo, and you saw the farm water pump. But if you lived in the country, you had a farm pump, because the water comes from the well. But the city people think it was just a fun little toy. But there was really water that comes out.

I teach my team this, so I think you're all going to get this. I say, "Business is like a farm pump. First, you take the handle, and you think it is ridiculous because there is no water coming out, and you believe there's nothing there. Then all of a sudden your arm starts hurting, but you are building pressure or your momentum. The well is building pressure, pressure, pressure. Guess what happens next? Boom, water comes out! When the water finally comes out, now you have what is called momentum. Once you reach this point the pressure in the well is so high, that you don't have to pump like a maniac anymore. Just a nice slow pump, and as long as you do this you're going to get all the water you need.

It's the same thing in business. So many times business people set this 90-day plan or a one-day plan done for 90 days, and they don't think there is any water in the well. They don't see enough sales. They don't see enough people coming in; they don't see enough, and they quit right before the water comes out. We teach this lesson all the time. The first 90 days you're building your pressure, or your momentum and the second 90 days you start to see more water. Some people making 20, 30, 40 thousand a month let go of their handle before they hit that peak production, and their business comes down, and they quit.

Chris Widener: It starts to atrophy a little bit and what they don't realize is that momentum allows your business to grow like what I call a "hockey stick." Think of it as an analogy from traditional investing; if you start putting $100 away every month when you are 20 years old, and you think to yourself well, I am not making that much money. At the end of the year you have $1200 plus maybe $200 in interest, and then you say, "Oh I only have $1400. I'm going to quit investing."

Anthony Powell: I think we have all done that.

Chris Widener: Exactly. What the successful people understand is that $100 put away every month from the time you are 20, your income goes like this: Think of this as a line. It is steady, and then you get to be 40, 50 and then you hit 60, and it goes like a hockey stick, slowly moving up and then a major turn up. The same is true in Network marketing. Some people that come right into a business and bam, they make money. I mean we all know people that came in and a year later they make a 30 grand a month.

Anthony Powell: They sign up that one hot person.

Chris Widener: But this is the exception, not the rule. The rule is you have to understand that this is about building momentum and it is kind of slow at first while you are building it. This is what will happen to your business: it stays relatively steady over a long period and if you stick with it, allow momentum to take over and ride the momentum; eventually, the income begins to grow. Your team goes from 1 to 4 to 8 to 16, and that feels slow, but eventually, it goes from 1000 to 2000 to 4000 to 8000 to 16000. That is momentum, and then you have an income that looks like a hockey stick.

Anthony Powell: And right here is where all of a sudden big money starts to come in. You have to go back and make sure you are doing your numbers to create momentum. But if you do the right numbers and create that moment, you are going to cash in. Then you know, the second part of it is to further it, and that means - and this is something my mentor taught me - once you start making 20, 30, 40 thousand a month, start reinvesting in your infrastructure because now you finally have money to build the business.

Most of the people like me start with a 473 credit score and a couple $100 to their name. I had no government hand out, no parent that gave me money, no credit card. I just want to play out momentum. I hope you guys get the hockey stick. It is real powerful. If we can give you anything, the sowing, the reaping, the attraction, the discipline, we would give you those things, the things that set up momentum, but if you don't understand that, you are going to have a hobby, and eventually you will go to the next hobby because you are just taking a hobby approach to it.

Chris Widener: Okay let's talk about law number five, the law of multiplication and duplication. Tell us about how important it is to multiply and to duplicate.

Anthony Powell: To understand this law you have to learn is the art of multiplication, and in our industry that means duplication. That means teaching people to do what you do, and when you multiply, you get more people. So you and somebody else have gotten two, and they find someone, you now have four. So what you are doing is you are compounding, you are multiplying your efforts. It is kind of like the penny a day story.

Chris Widener: Yeah, there is this whole thing where you get paid a penny the first day and if you doubled it every day, would you do your work for that? I can't remember the numbers exactly, but it goes 1 cent, 2 cents, 4 cents, 8 cents, so by the 5th day you looking at 16 cents but you don't realize it is like $1 million on day 31 or something crazy like that. If you think back to elementary school, the first piece of math you learned was addition, 8 plus 8 equals 16 right? But more powerful is learning multiplication, 8 times 8 is 64. So if you are just adding in your network marketing business, you will make some money, and you can make a nice little residual income. You can make $500 or $1000 a month, and that might pay for a new car or a vacation once a year but the real power, the real leverage, the exciting time, is when you get into multiplication.

Anthony Powell: When I was in my first company. Mark Hughes recognized me on stage, and I was at the position that typically doesn't earn the money that I was representing, and he says, "How did you make $14,000 last month at this level?" and I say, "Well it is real simple. I am retailing $20,000 a month of product." That means I had over 5000 customers on the product for retail. So Mark sits and says "Unbelievable." He recognized me in front of everybody as I was walking off the stage. He taught me something that changed my life, changed my business life. He's the owner of the company, a billionaire. He said, "I am real proud of you Anthony. Let me teach you how to build wealth right now. You are doing so great; your effort is incredible."

Chris Widener: You built income, but he wanted to teach you how to build wealth.

Anthony Powell: Right. So he said, "What I want you to do is don't retail $20,000 a month. I want you to retail about $2500 a month and then go find a lot of other people to retail $2500 a month, and you will make a fortune."

Chris Widener: You were operating out of addition. He wanted you to use the principle of multiplication, so you are doing a smaller number of personal volume, but you are then teaching other people how to do it and then that $2500 times a thousand or ten thousand people that's where you get that massive volume. It is multiplication instead of addition.

Anthony Powell: That's exactly right, and that's how you get the big checks. It's a lot of people doing small volume because you are not looking for some big hitter, you are just looking for a lot of people to do small volume or, said differently, multiplication, and that only comes from duplication.

Chris Widener: Some of the courses we are going to be coming out with are going to be talking about how to do multiplication and duplication.

Let's talk about law number six, the law of leadership and sales. This law was born out of a research project that I did with a bunch of top network marketers who were all making at least $100,000 a month. There was one leader that I asked, "How much time do you spend on your own business versus helping other people in their business?" It was interesting because she said that at the beginning of her career she spent about 90% of her time on her own business and about 10% on other people's business, but as the business grew, and then exploded, there was a shift. Now this top income earner said about 90% of her time is spent on other people's business and about 10% on her own business.

There is an interesting lesson here: Most people think they are going to become successful in network marketing by selling and a lot of people say, "I can't sell. I am not a salesperson," but the most powerful way of building massive wealth and bigger organizations is something different. The top skill set is not sales; it is leadership. It is not just selling to your group of people; it's about growing that massive volume, it is about becoming a leader and helping other people. So what are some of the leadership lessons that you learned as you transitioned out of selling and more into running this big organization that you have?

Anthony Powell: This is such a powerful section, and I am glad you brought it up here because when I started to build my business, I began to make a lot of money. Remember I talked about earlier the people that make $20,000 or $30,000 a month? They got a job, right? There are a couple of stages in this industry. The first is building mode and then once you build the foundation you go into what is called leader development mode. That's when you meet with your top producers, and you develop your skill set with them, so you spend more time with their business, more time critiquing their skill sets, more time developing their mindset, which ultimately develops your organization. Said differently, it gives you residual income.

Chris Widener: Yeah, imagine there are some people where they are the only leader, and everybody looks to the top. What would happen though if you became a leadership producing machine and built an organization of 10,000 people? Instead of just having one leader, you have leaders all the way down through the levels.

I had an interview once with John Kotter. He was the youngest guy ever to be tenured at Harvard Business School. He wrote a book called Leading Change, and I asked him, "What is the new cutting edge lesson on leadership that people need to know?" Not even missing a beat he said, "Leadership at every level of the organization. Successful organizations have leadership at every single level." So maybe you have a group of 10,000 people, and you are the leader, but you want people further down in your organization that maybe only have 4000 people, you want them to be a leader. You have to train them and take responsibility for raising up leaders. Then you want people who maybe only have 100 people in the organization, but you are teaching them how to become a leader, and it expands that organization and builds that massive kind of wealth people want.

Let's finish up with law number seven, the law of choice. Both successful and unsuccessful people are people who make choices every day. Every single day when you wake up, you are given choices. Sometimes there are two choices, sometimes there are ten choices, but it is about making the right choices.

Anthony Powell: Choices are about habits. Jim Rohn taught both of us that if you do something 13 days, the 14th day you create a habit, so that is a choice. You choose to do something every single day for 13, 14 days and then, bam; it's a habit. So if you want to get that, what do you do?

Chris Widener: Ice-cream 13 days in a row!

Anthony Powell: Boom! 13 days you can't stop, but you know, we are over-exaggerating a little bit, but that does happen to people. You know you are going to choose to sow and reap, you are going to choose to attract or not attract, you are going to attract people that are perhaps not what you want, like if you throw refrigerators in your front yard, you won't attract successful people. So if you got cars on the blocks in your front yard, you're not going to attract success. Either way, you have got to pay the price. You have to make sure you do it. Take momentum. You choose to create momentum or you don't choose to create momentum. You choose to multiply and duplicate, or you don't choose to multiply and duplicate. You choose to take your time and lead your leaders and develop them. That is a habit that you have to create as a leader in the finishing touches of your network marketing business.

Chris Widener: You know Dwight Eisenhower, the military general and then the President of the United States said, "The history of free men is never written by chance, but by choice: their choice." You have a choice each and every day; we thank you that you made the choice to read The 7 Laws of Network Marketing. We hope that you have learned some great information. You are going to now take this information because lots of people get information but don't use it. Then there are the people that are successful and make the choice to apply the information.

Anthony Powell: I would like to say thanks for choosing to be part of what we believe in. I will tell you this, that the next step for you is to either a) reread the book and get some more ownership about what we are teaching. I've read some books 13 times. I want the habit of what I have just learned. That is why I like the easy reads, the quick reads so that I can get all the golden nuggets out.

Chris Widener: It is very exciting to work with a guy like Anthony, and I have worked with other leaders as well. You have some people that are just about building their business. They make their money and do their own thing and then you have people, real difference makers like Anthony and some other folks that I have been able to be fortunate to work with, who have made their money and they can sit on a beach somewhere but don't. They help others.

The thing that I love about what Anthony and I are doing is that Anthony and I want to make a mark in the world. My big dream for my life is when I get to the end of my life is to know that I made a mark on the world. Anthony has done it; he's not one of those guys that just made something up. He has been in the trenches, built a massive business, and now he wants to help you do the kinds of things you need to do to build your own business. Get that time freedom, get that financial freedom, give your children a better life than you have, get a better lifestyle than you have, and make a mark in the world for yourself.

ABOUT AUTHORS

 Chris Widener is widely recognized as one of the top speakers in the world and was voted as one of the top 50 speakers in the world. Chris was mentored by and worked closely with legends Zig Ziglar and Jim Rohn, who called Chris "*The leader of the new generation of leadership and personal development experts.*" Chris is the author of 15 books and over 80 audio programs.

 A network marketing legend, Anthony Powell, started in the industry at the age of 19 and by the time he was 26 years old, was financially retired. Anthony eventually became one of the top income earners of all time in the industry. As a result of his leadership, many of those he's coached have gone on to become multiple 7 figure earners in the industry. If you're looking to go to the next level, here's your chance to work with a living legend.

CONGRATULATIONS

...now that you have finished
THE SEVEN LAWS OF NETWORK MARKETING, it's time to take
your business to the next level! **ELITE NETWORK MARKETER**
regularly offers **FREE WEBINARS** to help you go to the next
level and beyond. We are regularly scheduling amazing
new webinars on topics like:

- ✓ Establishing your **WHY**
- ✓ Finding your **TARGET MARKET**
- ✓ How to approach your **WARM** and **COLD MARKETS**
- ✓ How to gain **MASSIVE MOMENTUM**
- ✓ SOCIAL MEDIA
- ✓ PERSONAL DEVELOPMENT
- ✓ LEADERSHIP SKILLS
- ✓ Consistency and **DISCIPLINE**
- ✓ Provide **VALUE** to your prospects
- ✓ Law of **ATTRACTION**
- ✓ Never ending **STREAM OF LEADS**
- ✓ How to become a **GREAT LEADER**
- ✓ REPLICATION and DUPLICATION
- ✓ CLOSING PROSPECTS
- ✓ Running your business like a **BUSINESS**
- ✓ TIME MANAGEMENT
- ✓ Answering the "PYRAMID SCHEME" OBJECTION

So, get registered today! Get on over to
www.EliteNetworkMarketer.com/webinar
and get your free training today!

DISCOVER **ELITE CONVERSION PRO!**
THE COMPLETE ONLINE BUSINESS

Application for Affiliate Marketers

DRIVE TRAFFIC | CREATE LEADS | CONVERT SALES

Elite Conversion Pro is an **ONLINE BUSINESS SYSTEM**
that can be used for any company or product you're marketing.

You can run an **ONLINE BUSINESS** from a laptop or any mobile
device from anywhere in the world.

THIS INCLUDES:

- ✓ Automated **ONLINE SALES FUNNELS**
- ✓ **FUNNEL & WEBSITE BUILDER**
- ✓ Email and text **AUTORESPONDER**
- ✓ And an advanced **CONTACT MANAGEMENT SYSTEM**

Plus training from 7 figure internet
marketers and **"DONE FOR YOU"** traffic.

Start your **FREE TRIAL**
Go to **www.eliteconversionpro.com/ENM**

DISCOVER THE **SIMPLE 5 STEP** FACEBOOK AD FORMULA THAT **PRODUCED A 606% ROI!**

Get a **FREE** copy of the **FACEBOOK AD CHEAT SHEET**

Frustrated with Facebook ad results? Then grab a **FREE** copy of my **FACEBOOK AD CHEAT SHEET!**

In it, I reveal my simple 5 step Facebook ad formula that generated **$5000 IN SALES THE VERY FIRST WEEK** and went on to produce a staggering ROI!

 www.SocialLeadHack.net

JIM ROHN **LEGACY SERIES**

Through **The Jim Rohn Legacy Series**, Chris Widener imparts wisdom and knowledge gained through the seven years he was personally mentored by Jim Rohn. This audio program will give you a rare glimpse into the greatness of the man who was hailed as America's number one business philosopher.

Never before has a set of Rohn's best ideas been distilled into such a concise collection, like a 2.5-hour spa for the mind. Discover how to significantly improve your business, the top eight principles that will act as a road map in your quest to achieve greatness, and three network marketing philosophies that million-dollar earners use every day.

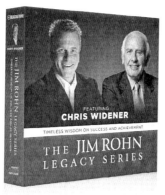

Available from
http://amzn.to/2ltpftl

THE CASE FOR NETWORK MARKETING

Chris Widener, one of America's Top Business Minds, provides a simple explanation on the power of one of the world's most unique and misunderstood businesses today. Take an in-depth look at Network Marketing through a comparison of traditional businesses. Discover how an MLM business has unlimited power to produce wealth.

The Case for Network Marketing will show you that it doesn't matter where you start, or whether you have a college degree. In this profit system, Chris Widener clearly illustrates this unique opportunity to become famously wealthy.

Quantity Price Breaks for Prospecting Booklet

Units	Pricing
1 to 4	$7.99
5 to 10	$5.00
11 to 24	$4.00
25 to 99	$3.00
100+	$2.50

Contact Made for Success Publishing to order:
(425) 657-0300
service@madeforsuccess.net

Available from
ChrisWidener.com and bookstores everywhere.